NORTH AMERICAN ANIMALS

American Robins

by Megan Borgert-Spaniol

BLASTOFF!
READERS
3

BELLWETHER MEDIA • MINNEAPOLIS, MN

Note to Librarians, Teachers, and Parents:

Blastoff! Readers are carefully developed by literacy experts and combine standards-based content with developmentally appropriate text.

Level 1 provides the most support through repetition of high-frequency words, light text, predictable sentence patterns, and strong visual support.

Level 2 offers early readers a bit more challenge through varied simple sentences, increased text load, and less repetition of high-frequency words.

Level 3 advances early-fluent readers toward fluency through increased text and concept load, less reliance on visuals, longer sentences, and more literary language.

Level 4 builds reading stamina by providing more text per page, increased use of punctuation, greater variation in sentence patterns, and increasingly challenging vocabulary.

Level 5 encourages children to move from "learning to read" to "reading to learn" by providing even more text, varied writing styles, and less familiar topics.

Whichever book is right for your reader, Blastoff! Readers are the perfect books to build confidence and encourage a love of reading that will last a lifetime!

This edition first published in 2017 by Bellwether Media, Inc.

No part of this publication may be reproduced in whole or in part without written permission of the publisher. For information regarding permission, write to Bellwether Media, Inc., Attention: Permissions Department, 5357 Penn Avenue South, Minneapolis, MN 55419.

Library of Congress Cataloging-in-Publication Data

Names: Borgert-Spaniol, Megan, 1989- author.
Title: American Robins / by Megan Borgert-Spaniol.
Description: Minneapolis, MN : Bellwether Media, Inc., [2017] | Series:
   Blastoff! Readers: North American Animals | Audience: Age 5-8. |
   Audience: K to Grade 3. | Includes bibliographical references and index.
Identifiers: LCCN 2015046392 | ISBN 9781626174009 (hardcover : alk. paper)
Subjects: LCSH: American robin–Juvenile literature.
Classification: LCC QL696.P288 B67 2017 | DDC 598.8/42–dc23
LC record available at http://lccn.loc.gov/2015046392

Printed in the United States of America, North Mankato, MN.

Table of Contents

What Are American Robins?

American robins are a type of **thrush**. They are the most common thrushes in North America.

N
W E
S

American robin range =
conservation status: least concern

Extinct

Extinct in the Wild

Critically Endangered

Endangered

Vulnerable

Near Threatened

Least Concern

The birds live in trees and bushes in yards, parks, and fields. They are also found in woodlands, mountains, and **tundras**.

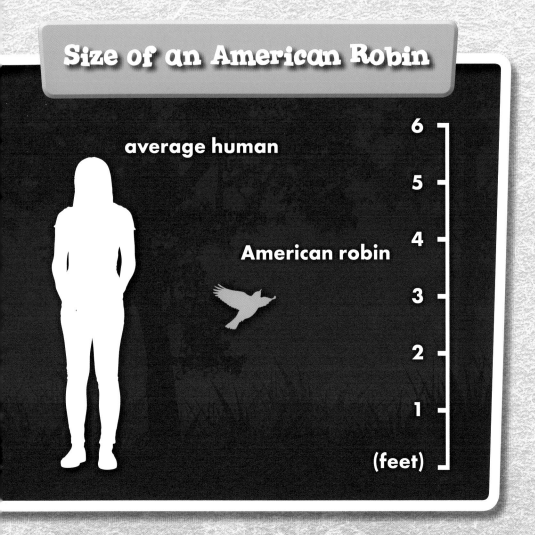

Size of an American Robin

average human

American robin

6
5
4
3
2
1
(feet)

American robins are the largest thrushes in North America. They measure about 10 inches (25 centimeters) long.

Their **wingspan** is about
14 inches (36 centimeters) wide.

The birds have plump orange bellies and yellow beaks. Their backs and tails are gray or brown.

Identify an American Robin

gray or brown feathers

orange belly

yellow beak

Males are often darker than females. However, they can be hard to tell apart.

American robins are known for their cheerful birdsong.

They often begin to sing before sunrise. They continue to sing throughout the day!

Finding Food

American robins search for food during the daytime. They run or hop across the ground.

Then they stop and stand still. This is how they spot **prey**.

earthworms

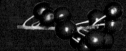

chokecherries

juniper berries

dogwood berries

American grasshoppers

beetle grubs

The robins are **omnivores**. In winter, they eat a lot of berries.

In summer, they like to eat
earthworms. They also feed on
insects, spiders, and snails.

American robins form **flocks** during winter. Some flocks **migrate** to warmer areas.

blue jays

American crows

black rat snakes

red squirrels

Cooper's hawks

house cats

Flocks may gather in trees to eat and **roost**. The birds warn one another when **predators** are near.

Nests and Babies

Females lay eggs two or three times each year. They build nests out of grasses, twigs, and mud.

The females sit in the nests to keep the eggs warm until they hatch.

Parents feed chicks insects and earthworms. After about two weeks, the chicks leave the nest. **Fledglings** stay under bushes until they are ready to fly!

Name for babies:	chicks
Number of eggs laid:	3 to 5 eggs
Time spent inside egg:	12 to 14 days
Time spent with parents:	about 2 weeks

Glossary

fledglings—young birds that have feathers for flight

flocks—groups of American robins that travel and roost together

migrate—to travel from one place to another, often with the seasons

omnivores—animals that eat both plants and animals

predators—animals that hunt other animals for food

prey—animals that are hunted by other animals for food

roost—to rest or sleep

thrush—a type of small or medium-sized songbird

tundras—dry lands where the ground is frozen year-round

wingspan—the distance between the tip of one wing to the tip of the other

To Learn More

AT THE LIBRARY

Alderfer, Jonathan K. *National Geographic Kids Bird Guide of North America: The Best Birding Book for Kids from National Geographic's Bird Experts.* Washington, D.C.: National Geographic, 2013.

Amstutz, Lisa J. *Robins.* North Mankato, Minn.: Capstone Press, 2016.

Schuetz, Kari. *Birds.* Minneapolis, Minn.: Bellwether Media, 2013.

ON THE WEB

Learning more about American robins is as easy as 1, 2, 3.

1. Go to www.factsurfer.com.

2. Enter "American robins" into the search box.

3. Click the "Surf" button and you will see a list of related web sites.

With factsurfer.com, finding more information is just a click away.

Index